Recovering from a traumatic birth – a practical guide

Alexandra Heath

Copyright © 2020 Alexandra Heath
All rights reserved.
ISBN:

DEDICATION

This book is dedicated to the many courageous parents that I have worked with and who have inspired me to share what I know is possible when it comes to recovering from a difficult or traumatic birth experience.

CONTENTS

	Acknowledgments	I
1	How to use this book	1
2	Did you experience a difficult birth or pre- or post-natal event?	Pg 4
3	Why does past trauma continue to hurt now? Understanding your experience from an emotional, physiological and neurological point of view	Pg 15
4	An anxiety toolkit: the basics	Pg 32
5	Unpacking what happened, how you felt then, and how it feels now: An exercise to bring clarity and understanding	Pg 44
6	Getting acknowledgement and validation of your traumatic experience	Pg 49
7	How would you like things to be different, if you could choose? Using a solution-focused approach	Pg 54
8	Breaking the patterns and making space for new ways of thinking, feeling and responding	Pg 61

Recovering from a traumatic birth – a practical guide

9   Planning for a better birth next time   Pg 79

ACKNOWLEDGMENTS

Thanks to Saphia Fleury my editor who brought clarity and good sense to the process of writing a practical guide.

1 HOW TO USE THIS BOOK

This book is for anyone who has experienced a difficult or traumatic event along their journey to parenthood. This commonly means birth trauma but can also include other difficult, stressful or even life-threatening events such as miscarriage, baby loss, premature labour and birth, having an unwell baby, poor postnatal care or a difficult feeding experience.

This list is not exhaustive. I have supported many women traumatised by lengthy, invasive IVF treatments, severe hyperemesis (sickness), birth injury and other unrelated but serious illness experienced during pregnancy or the postnatal period.

After any difficult or traumatic event it can be common to feel the lasting impact of that experience on our emotional health. This can, in turn, negatively affect day-to-day life. As well as struggling to cope with everyday life, many people also face the additional challenge of caring for an infant and maybe other children and family too. Looking after others can feel onerous and heavy when we ourselves are struggling with residual anxiety from any traumatic event. The old adage of 'you cannot pour from an empty cup' is never truer than when it comes to looking after babies and children. My hope is that this book and the exercises within can provide some space to begin processing what has happened. I hope that a new understanding about your experiences can restore some peace and calm to your mind, and ultimately have a positive impact on other areas of your life.

The exercises mentioned in this book are designed to support you as you take a step towards acknowledging your feelings about what happened and how your experience continues to affect your life. You are invited to join a closed Facebook group of people who are also reading this book and are using the exercises. This community can provide support, insight and inspiration as you work towards feeling better.

The exercises are designed to be approached in order as you work through the book. The exception is the first relaxation exercise which can be used straight away to create a relaxed state. Used on their own and outside of the book's context the other exercises will make little sense and will not be as effective.

Recovering from a traumatic event isn't always a linear process. Many people feel a great deal better after initially confronting their feelings, but may then be re-triggered and feel as though they have been dragged backwards again. I hope, however, that the resources shared within this book can sustain and support you as these discoveries are made and as you move forward (and sometimes backwards again!) It is important for you to know that you are not alone, that what happened is not your fault, and that you can recover and feel differently with the right guidance and support.

You can gain access to the closed Facebook group and the other exercises and resources here
https://traumaticbirthrecovery.com/book-resources/

Recovering from a traumatic birth – a practical guide

2: DID YOU EXPERIENCE A DIFFICULT BIRTH OR PRE- OR POST-NATAL EVENT?

Have your experiences during pregnancy, birth or the post-natal months affected you so greatly that they still have an impact on your day-to-day life? Look at the list of symptoms and feelings below, and consider how many of them apply to you.

- Do you constantly think about what happened and find that this rumination brings you to tears or makes you feel angry or anxious?
- Do you find it difficult to talk about your experience because it is too upsetting?
- Do you avoid situations where birth might be discussed, like mum and baby groups or chats with friends and family?
- Is this avoidance isolating you and making you feel lonely?
- Do you worry excessively whenever a woman close to you is due to give birth?
- Do you feel jumpy and on edge?
- Are you uncomfortable about leaving your baby with other people?

Recovering from a traumatic birth – a practical guide

- Are you too nervous to put your baby down or leave them alone, even for a moment?
- Do you have intrusive and disturbing thoughts about something bad happening to your baby?
- Do you blame your partner, midwife or care provider for what happened to you?
- Do you experience anger that is all-consuming, tiring and affecting your relationships?
- Do you sense the unwelcome, constant presence of anxiety, unease and fear but don't really understand why you feel this way?
- Have you experienced flashbacks or nightmares about the event?
- Do you feel guilty and to blame about what happened?
- Do you feel resentful and jealous when you hear about other peoples positive birth experiences?
- Are the strong, raw and intense feelings about what happened impacting on your relationships?

This is certainly not an exhaustive list of symptoms and feelings that can remain after a difficult or traumatic birth, but they represent common experiences among the women and families I have supported over the years.

"I thought that I just had post-partum depression because I wasn't handling it well. Out of nowhere I was having flashes, I was nervous all the time. I was so afraid something was going to happen and that we would be separated again."
– Kristen

Recovering from a traumatic birth – a practical guide

"When I was nine months postpartum I basically had a breakdown. I blamed myself for not coping. Why did I find it all so difficult? Why can't I get over it or get on with it?"
– Gemma

"It turned out that the anaesthetist had punctured my dura cavity while administering the spinal mid-contraction, meaning my spinal fluid was draining away. Weeks later I had to go back in with secondary post-partum haemorrhaging, where some placenta had been left behind. During this procedure they punctured my uterus. The whole experience sent me into a bit of depression, which I'm only just recovering from."
– Lauren

"I was terrified, absolutely terrified. I ended up with a prolapsed bowel and bladder and I was absolutely devastated. I was as low as a person could be."
–Marie.

"I know I am not me and I know I am not well, but I need you to put up with me."
– Charlotte

These symptoms and heavy feelings can become exhausting and may make the already challenging situation of caring for an infant feel like a constant struggle to cope.

Maybe you have already been offered support, and hopefully you have a compassionate family who can care for you and offer comfort and a loving space to heal.

Recovering from a traumatic birth – a practical guide

However, this often isn't the case, and even loved ones may struggle to provide the compassion, time and patience that you need to heal. Sometimes it is those closest to us who appear to be most hurtful and unfeeling, as they urge you to 'move on', 'get over it' or 'stop talking about it'.

Unfortunately, this sentiment can be echoed by care providers with platitudes such as 'what matters is that you have a healthy baby', or 'you can try for a natural birth / VBAC next time' – there is often a lot of talk about 'next time'! The subtexts here are 'you are unimportant' and 'we made a hash of your birth this time, but maybe next time we'll do better'.

These minimizing and dismissing statements that parents often hear from healthcare professionals can leave them feeling like they are at fault or have failed at birth. The very opposite is true when the system has failed to provide a safe place for parents to birth.

In truth, I think it is difficult to find the right people who can offer the understanding, acknowledgement and peace that you are probably seeking right now. Often there are no words that can truly offer solace. People may try to comfort, placate or soothe you. However, I believe that being really heard and understood may be of more value to you at these times.

Your story is important. You are important, and what happened to you should not have happened. I would like to reassure you that if you have feelings of injustice, anger and sadness about your experience then these emotions are completely valid and normal, given what you have been through.

Birthing should be a normal, physiological life event 90% of the time, according to the World Health Organization. However, most parents are unprepared for the modern, 21st Century birth experience, which for the vast majority of people takes place in a hospital. In this institutional setting, birth is frequently reduced to a mechanical process of getting the baby out using the most expedient means, without regard for the long-term price paid by the mother, father and baby. Many parents leave hospital feeling man handled and processed like a meat in a packing factory, battered and bruised emotionally and physically. They are expected to return home and function adequately enough to care for a baby, when in truth, many folk just want to curl up and cry over the ordeal that they have suffered.

I wish that, by now, we could have found a better way to birth that doesn't mean having to trade-off safe delivery of the baby with a good outcome for parents. Too often, trauma occurs because the baby's safety is used as a reason to transgress the physical and emotional boundaries of parents. In the words of Birthrights founder Elizabeth Prochaska, "the woman is not a suitcase". Yet, once the baby is out, some women are treated like spent commodities that have passed their usefulness. Hence the insulting platitudes so often used to silence parents such as 'what matters most is that you have a healthy baby'.

Given the inadequacies of the current system, it would not be surprising or unreasonable to be consumed with anger about what has taken place. This is completely understandable and justifiable if you have been let down by those who are supposed to serve and support you at this vulnerable and often stressful time. Some women experience this as a loss, and culturally we have some unhelpful ways of thinking, and talking, about loss. The healthcare system can appear hostile and uncaring. It exists to deal with the physical side of reproduction and birth, but can appear absent of any human understanding about what it means to lose out on a good, dignified birth, or a full pregnancy, or a healthy baby. Often people report feeling jealous anger towards those who have had what they were deprived of (a good birth experience, a healthy pregnancy, or the experience of motherhood). Unfortunately, this is also part and parcel of the natural but painful period of grief that can follow a traumatic perinatal event.

Feelings of anger and guilt, although understandable and completely natural, can be exhausting and overwhelming, and consume a lot of mental space and energy. Anger can raise levels of the stress hormone cortisol, cause physical and emotional tension, and supress levels of the 'love hormone' oxytocin. All of this is ultimately unhelpful when trying to care for a baby, come to terms with a loss, or cope with a subsequent pregnancy. Because anger is such an all-consuming emotion, it deprives us of feeling much else, robbing us of the precious opportunity to enjoy our families and our parenting experience. This in turn may feel like another injustice, which can further fuel anger and create a seemingly never ending cycle of resentment and, or guilt too.

Recovering from a traumatic birth – a practical guide

I believe that understanding your emotions, your ways of thinking and your responses to the experience is the key to freeing yourself from their exhausting and ultimately destructive power. While it is completely natural to feel the way that you do, it is unhelpful because it deprives you of feeling peaceful, calm and joyful about your parenting experience now. Let's face it – raising a young family can be challenging enough, without being saddled with heavy feelings like anger and grief. It is so much easier to navigate the choppy waters of parenthood without that extra weight of intense, negative emotion. Sometimes people feel stuck in the emotions of anger and resentment because on many levels they are often justified. However, if you are reading this book, there is also probably a large part of you that also feels that these feelings are quite wearing to live with and perhaps you would like to be free of them. In these situations it can help to give yourself permission to feel differently, even though that can feel incredibly challenging and sometimes conflicting to do so. It can be a starting point to acknowledge that your feelings are natural and valid given what you have been through but they are not serving you or your life right now.

Admittedly, it can be hard to feel like you have a choice when these strong emotions are owning you, when feelings are compulsive and can be re-triggered without any warning. This immersive and overwhelming wave of toxic emotion can feel jarring and unfair during what is expected to be a 'happy time' of your life. You may also be confused about why you feel the way you do. Making sense of these feelings is a necessary part of the healing process. But for now, the first step towards recovery is *wanting* to feel differently, and acknowledging that this is possible. Right now, all you need to do is trust this tried-and-tested process to guide you through a series of exercises that can bring you clarity, calm and hope for the future.

You may be doubting your own experience at this point, asking yourself if you are just being 'a bit dramatic'. Some parents might start to wonder 'was it even that bad anyway?' They may think 'I'm fine, my baby is fine, so why am I still so upset by what happened?', or 'I had a natural birth so I should be pleased, right?' The feelings that can remain after a difficult birth experience often have more to do with how you felt during that experience and less to do with what actually happened. This does not make the feelings less valid, or real.

I have met many parents over the years who have faced serious medical emergencies during or following birth, but who nevertheless made a full recovery, both mentally and emotionally, because they felt well-cared for, respected and listened to. Conversely, I have also met many parents who, on paper, appeared to have had straightforward deliveries, but who were traumatised by the poor care they received. These parents had often experienced high levels of fear and anxiety during birth. They may even have feared for their life or their baby's life; certainly for their safety. These feelings of being 'unsafe' in the hospital environment were sometimes the result of unkind treatment given by care providers, but were often the result of standard hospital policies such as induction or vaginal examinations, or being declined pain relief in labour.

Recovering from a traumatic birth – a practical guide

These births might look 'normal' and perhaps had a good outcome for the baby, but nevertheless they left a devastating mark on the families because standard medical interventions were applied in a manner than took something of these folks' humanity. Feelings of transgression, being 'done to', and of boundaries being crossed are very understandable given the nature of some of these standard hospital procedures, especially when they are suggested in the context of being needed 'for your baby's health and safety'. This way of presenting the necessity of carrying out a procedure leaves parents very vulnerable to experiencing their birth as traumatic, since it removes any real choice. It is likely that, as a result of this communication from the healthcare provider to the parents, that the parents will perceive a threat to life, either for themselves or their baby, a breach of their physical boundaries, and a breach of their autonomy. The breach of physical boundaries can come about during procedures such as vaginal examinations, insertion of catheters and intravenous lines, and use of foetal heart monitors. Breaches of autonomy occur since you can't just choose to get up and leave, and because interventions are often not presented as a choice. These situations would be very stressful for most people. For many parents, such experiences come as a shock because they simply had no idea that giving birth would be this way. It is also confusing for parents, because care providers treat the situation as normal and routine. This can present a surreal experience for parents who have encountered care that felt very wrong but which was nevertheless treated as normal by their care-givers, leaving them to question their own experiences and judgement.

Recovering from a traumatic birth – a practical guide

On top of any emotional pain, perhaps you have also been left with a physical injury because of your birth. Injuries to women during childbirth are incredibly common and also unhelpfully taboo. The stigma and medical ignorance surrounding maternal birth injuries can compound the trauma of sustaining such an injury, since it means that women may have incredible difficulties getting a diagnosis and accessing treatment. Reports of women being gaslighted by their GP when they seek advice about their birth injury and the resulting problems (prolapse, incontinence and painful sex) are sadly far too common. If you are currently experiencing this issue with your care provider then please seek a second opinion or contact the charity MASIC[1] to find your nearest assessment clinic. An injury of this nature can constitute an ongoing trauma as women struggle to get the right diagnosis, treatment and care. Subsequent visits to hospital and engagement with healthcare staff can re-trigger the original birth trauma and be a new source of trauma as this area of the body is physically revisited time and time again.

If you have experienced a physical trauma on top of emotional trauma resulting from birth, and you feel that this physical trauma is unresolved, then you can still benefit from the exercises in this book. Be extra gentle with yourself and use the support available through the Facebook group, found in the resources section https://traumaticbirthrecovery.com/book-resources/ as you navigate the exercises.

[1] MASIC stands for Mothers with Anal Sphincter Injuries in Childbirth. See https://masic.org.uk/

Recovering from a traumatic birth – a practical guide

This book can also help if you didn't give much thought to your birth at the time or postnatally, but are now pregnant again and feel traumatised by the thought of having to endure another birth. Maybe you can feel your anxiety increasing as your due date approaches, as if you are walking back into a potential nightmare. This book can help you to unpick those feelings, understand them, quell them, and ultimately plan for a better birth next time.

"What I would really like to be able to do is to recall and reflect on the time when my children were small without that pain and that anger."
– Marie

3. Why does past trauma continue to hurt now?
Understanding your experience from an emotional,
physiological and neurological point of view

What happened months, or even years, ago can still grip us with strong emotion despite the passage of time. This can feel very confusing, and as a result we may attribute different meanings to past events in an attempt to understand why they still hurt us. So, for example, you may have had thoughts like:

"What happened to me was unjust. It continues to haunt me because it was so unfair."

"I have always been let down by other people, so this was just another example of that. I believe people will always let me down, and that's what hurts so much."

No doubt it has occurred to you that it is unhelpful to still have these feelings, thoughts and responses today. This is especially true if they are robbing you of other more joyful feelings, peaceful thoughts and easier ways of responding that would better serve you and your family's happiness. Nonetheless, it is completely natural to sometimes feel arrested by the strength of these feelings, compelled by them and unable to stop them. Do you recognise any of the feelings below?

- My past experience still affects me up in ways that I wish it didn't.
- I avoid certain situations, making my life feel small and limited in opportunity.
- My feelings affect the way that I relate to my partner, or child and they have driven a wedge between us.
- My experience has affected my sense of self, damaged my self-confidence and left me feeling less of myself.
- I have learnt to habituate these crappy ways of thinking and feeling about myself.
- I feel ashamed about what happened to me.
- This is just the way I am now. I just get on with it, and have made allowances for this new way of being.

Even if you have accommodated these changes, I want to suggest that you don't have to tolerate them. And if you could go back to being you, to having the relationship with your partner that you once enjoyed, and begin to experience a joyful, peaceful life with your family, would you choose that instead? I quite understand if this seems far-fetched or an impossible state to get to from where you are now. But the first step is to desire a change and then to believe that it is possible.

Recovering from a traumatic birth – a practical guide

The exercises in this book will help you to discover your own innate ability to heal, recover and thrive. These exercises will involve an examination of how you felt then and continue to feel now, which can feel scary. However, there is a whole community of parents online waiting to hold your hand, support you and provide inspiration in the closed Facebook group. You can find the details on joining here https://traumaticbirthrecovery.com/book-resources/

I also believe that a little knowledge can bring a lot of power. Understanding why you continue to feel so bad is an important step in healing. Your way of understanding your trauma is valid; it is your experience and yours alone, after all.

However, did you also know that there is a neurological reason why incidents in the past continue to hurt now? This is directly connected to what takes place in the brain during a traumatic event.

When we are in a frightening situation, perhaps one where we fear for our life or safety, or the life or safety of someone very dear to us, it is naturally a very stressful event. Everyone is programmed to find this kind of situation difficult and stressful. During pregnancy or birth, this is compounded by the fact that we can't escape by running away (although we may desperately want to) and that we may feel completely powerless to influence or change the situation. We have lost all agency. There may also be an aspect of being transgressed (being 'done to') that makes us feel very unsafe at that point in time.

Recovering from a traumatic birth – a practical guide

While this highly stressful event is underway, the brain and nervous system senses that you feel in danger and triggers what is commonly known as the 'fight or flight or freeze' response (more scientifically known as the sympathetic (stress) response). This physiological response is triggered by the area of the brain responsible for stress: the amygdala. Your amygdala is trying to protect you from what it has perceived as a threat to life, and will send a message to all of the other organs in your body, telling them to get you out of that situation as quickly as possible. Your body will release adrenalin to facilitate super-human action: your heart will beat faster to pump blood to the larger muscle groups that will carry you away from danger and your breathing will become rapid to transport more oxygen via the blood to these muscles. The amygdala takes over your brain function, limiting the functioning of the 'higher brain' (the prefrontal cortex). This is no time for logic, it is time for ACTION! The amygdala continues to sound the alarm to GET OUT, and if its commands are not honoured then it won't give up. As the amygdala rages, and the (perceived) life-threatening event continues, the various aspects of the event become inextricably linked to the amygdala via another area of the brain, the hippocampus. In effect, these stimuli become imprinted on your brain as images and sensations. They may include images of the hospital room, the midwife or the consultant obstetrician, a feeling of penetration, the word "push", the smell of the nurse's perfume, the image of your baby or birth partner, or anything else present. These sensory aspects become stored in the hippocampus, and whenever they are present again they trip off the same alarm in the amygdala, flooding the body with adrenalin. Each time,

Recovering from a traumatic birth – a practical guide

your heart will race, your breathing will speed up, and you will once again feel very uneasy and unsafe.

We are biologically programmed, therefore, to relive the anxiety and fear every time we are reminded of the traumatic event. This may include simply remembering the experience or talking about it, or physically encountering any of these stimuli (sights, sounds, sensations, smells) again. Every time the amygdala is re-triggered then the neural pathway between the hippocampus and the amygdala becomes strengthened. It is for this reason that talking therapies are limited in their ability to lift trauma symptoms. Although a trauma informed listening service can provide acknowledgment and validation of your experience and feelings they can also drive the symptoms of trauma deeper if they focus solely on what happened. The constant re-telling and remembering of any trauma can strengthen the connections between the memory and the trauma response, unfortunately holding recovery at bay.

For this reason, any pleas to "just forget about it" or "move on" are biologically impossible, since it is our own natural brain functioning that makes it difficult to move on from a traumatic event.

Sometimes, once a difficult or traumatic event ends, a person's nervous system returns to its normal relaxed state and they are able to get on with their life. They do their best to forget what happened and re-engage with day-to-day activities. They appear to have made a full recovery.

However, if this doesn't happen, and the autonomic nervous system stays in a state of high arousal, it is as though a light has remained switched on. The person experiencing this is held in a 'fight or flight' trauma state, feeling unsafe, anxious and hyper-vigilant of their surroundings.

Living day-to-day with the brain's fight or flight system activated is draining and exhausting. It can also lead to other health problems because the constant state of alert suppresses the body's immune system. One way that people try to cope with these high levels of anxiety, upset and tension in the body is through self-medication with drink or drugs. This attempt to cope with the difficult feelings and symptoms of trauma is obviously unhelpful long term.

Even when women have been able to recover and return to normality after a traumatic birth, sometimes their trauma is re-triggered by another pregnancy and they find that symptoms once again begin to invade their life with breath-taking impact.

Some people become determined to resist the upset caused by stimuli that trigger their trauma, and do their upmost to avoid all reminders, conversations or thoughts about the traumatic event. This denial and avoidance of symptoms is often masked as 'wanting to move on' or 'forget'. However, this approach can also lead to a feeling of numbness about the event. The problem with numbing our feelings about one event is that, very often, this numbing extends to *all* feelings, not just unpleasant ones.

Recovering from a traumatic birth – a practical guide

All of these ways of experiencing symptoms (immediate and delayed responses, re-triggering stimuli and avoidance) are completely natural responses to what was a very difficult, stressful, maybe even life-threatening situation. You have nothing to fear and no reason to feel shame or guilt for trying to cope in the best way that you can. How you feel is a completely natural and normal response to what was an abnormally difficult, stressful and traumatic event. Birth is not meant to be this bad; it is the highly medicalised yet under-funded approach to birth that has made it so for many people.

The following table shows the myriad of different trauma symptoms that can be experienced by a person following a traumatic birth.

The categories of symptoms in this table are taken from the City Birth Trauma Scale developed by Susan Ayers specifically for the diagnosis of birth trauma.

Intrusions	Avoidance symptoms	Negative mood and cognitions	Hyperarousal
Flashbacks to the birth and/or reliving the experience	Trying to avoid thinking about the birth	Not able to remember details of the birth	Feeling irritable or aggressive
Recurrent thoughts or	Trying to avoid things that remind	Feeling negative about myself	Feeling self-destructive or acting recklessly

Recovering from a traumatic birth – a practical guide

Intrusions	Avoidance symptoms	Negative mood and cognitions	Hyperarousal
memories of the birth that can't be controlled	me of the birth (e.g., people, places, TV programmes)	Thinking something awful will happen	Feeling jumpy or easily startled
Getting upset when reminded of the birth		Blaming myself or others for what happened during the birth	Feeling tense and on edge
Bad dreams or nightmares about the birth (or related to the birth)		Feeling strong negative emotions about the birth (e.g., fear, anger, shame)	Not sleeping well because of things that are not due to the baby's sleep pattern
		Lost interest in activities that were important	

Recovering from a traumatic birth – a practical guide

Intrusions	Avoidance Symptoms	Negative mood & cognitions	Hyperarousal
		Feeling detached from other people	Problems concentrating
		Not able to feel positive emotions (e.g., happy, excited)	Feeling emotionally numb

It is important to understand these symptoms as a normal response to a really difficult, often life threatening (even if only perceived) situation. As such, I belief that trauma symptoms are more helpfully thought of as a psychological injury than a mental illness.

Living day-to-day with these symptoms, however, can take its toll as you struggle to cope with the impact on your life, your relationships and your sense of self.

Experiencing anxiety and panic on a daily basis is exhausting and all-consuming and eventually robs us of confidence and hope for the future. High levels of stress take away all of our energy at a time when huge demands are being made on us by our new baby. When we are thrown into this survival mode, caring for others becomes very difficult. That job is made even harder when we feel constantly under threat.

Anger and jealousy are destructive emotions which can poison relationships and damage families' potential futures together. Shame and guilt are equally destructive as they contribute to feelings of unworthiness and low self-esteem.

I believe that, left unaddressed, trauma symptoms can develop into more entrenched mental health problems as a person adapts to cope with the weight of these feelings every day. Many of these coping mechanisms are ultimately harmful. Addiction problems can arise when drink or drugs are used to temporarily turn down the volume on anxiety and to numb feelings of pain. Obsessive and compulsive rituals (leading to Obsessive Compulsive Disorder – OCD) can be a way of feeling safe and in control when everyday anxiety and fear become intolerable. Feelings of chronic unworthiness and loss of hope, moreover, can lead to depression.

In my work as a Clinical Hypnotherapist I always ask 'when did this problem (addiction, OCD, anxiety or depression) begin?' Most often, the person in front of me can pinpoint the exact event that caused the symptoms which led these negative coping mechanisms.

Dealing with the symptoms of trauma before they reach this stage is undoubtedly much easier than unravelling them later on. However, if you feel that you are already moving towards an unhealthy coping strategy, or already have one, then rest assured that the exercises in this book can still help.

Understanding the neurological impact of trauma

Although we each have a unique experience of what happens to us, and a unique way of responding to that experience, we all share the same neurobiology for processing events and the feelings associated with them.

So we are all unique, yet we all share the same biology.

Why is this important?

I believe that, if we each understood how difficult events affect us as individuals, not only would we be more inclined to adopt more humane systems in society (the way in which we give birth being one of those systems) but we would also know how to heal ourselves and care for others who are affected.

There are two parts of the brain that are important to our basic understanding of what happens when we experience a threat to our life or safety, or that of someone close to us. As we saw above, the amygdala is the part of our brain responsible for our survival, and which gives the signal to the rest of the body to flee a perceived harm. The amygdala is a very small, almond-shaped area of the mid-brain (amygdala is derived from the Greek word for almond). It is thought to be one of the most primitive parts of our brain. As such, the amygdala doesn't recognised the subtleties of your situation. Once danger has been perceived, it doesn't stop commanding action until action is taken. So, for example, if a period of time passes without the danger coming to fruition, the amygdala still won't stand down. It will continue to sound the alarm until it is honoured.

The cascade of physiological responses set in motion by the amygdala (fast heart rate, shallow and rapid breathing, tense muscles, flooding the body with adrenaline and catecholamine stress hormones) is coupled with a narrowing-down of brain function that causes difficulty in problem-solving or finding a logical way out of the situation. This physiological response is very unhelpful to the natural unfolding of birth, and can even bring the process to a complete – albeit temporary – halt.

It is important to understand that the threat does not have to be real for the fight or flight response to be activated. It just has to be perceived. Misunderstanding this vital difference has led to a huge gap in healthcare providers' understanding of perinatal trauma, its causes and effects.

For many healthcare providers, routine protocol and procedures such as continuous foetal monitoring, vaginal examinations and inductions, for example, are just part and parcel of their everyday working life in a maternity ward. The problem lies in how these protocols and procedures are often communicated to parents. Too often, these common procedures are explained to parents as necessary for the good of their babies' health or wellbeing. This immediately puts in parents minds that something is 'wrong', or that there could be 'danger' ahead for the mother or baby. As a result, many standard healthcare procedures leave parents vulnerable to experiencing birth as a traumatic event.

Paradoxically, parents often think that a medical environment is safest because they hear so many traumatic birth stories where medical intervention was required. They wrongly attribute the cause of the trauma to something that went wrong with birth, or with the woman's body, rather than there being something wrong with the system itself.

With the amygdala dominating the brain and commanding action, a neural pathway is formed between the amygdala and the short-term memory store of the brain, the hippocampus (which is named after the Greek word for seahorse, which it resembles in shape). This neural pathway is a physical and biological connection between the memory of the traumatic event and the fight or flight response.

As a result, even after the traumatic event has passed, memories of the event will re-trigger the fight or flight response all over again. Not only does this happen each time the event is remembered, but also whenever a sensory cue is present. These sensory cues, or stimuli, can include seeing a birth on TV, hearing a certain word, or smelling the 'hospital smell', for example. Every time the neural pathways between the hippocampus and the amygdala are triggered, the pathway becomes stronger and more entrenched. This is why talking therapies alone can be of limited value for trauma treatment, unless they are 'trauma informed' they risk strengthening the trauma response.

Recovering from a traumatic birth – a practical guide

Unfortunately, recurrent thoughts, flashbacks and 'reliving' the experience are also recognised symptoms of trauma. This means that a person undergoing these symptoms can be forced to recollect what happened over and over again.

Trauma symptoms therefore have a neurobiological explanation. Yet for many people experiencing these symptoms, it is easy to attribute further meaning to the experience. This may include thoughts like:

'Why do these awful things always happen to me?'

'I am worthless – that's why this happened to me.'

'Why did no one protect me?'

Although it is understandable that some people might attribute these kinds of meaning to an event, it is rarely helpful in overcoming trauma symptoms.

Self-blame and guilt are common feelings experienced after a difficult or traumatic birth experience. Parents often berate themselves harshly and, when reflecting on the experience, ask themselves constantly 'why didn't I say no, or tell them to stop?'

In my previous role as a doula who has attended many births (including, sadly, a few traumatic ones) I have seen how difficult it is for labouring women to speak up. This reluctance or inability to speak up extends to birth partners and even, sometimes, to myself as a doula. We are all vulnerable to being caught up in the stress and perceived danger of the moment. It can be incredibly hard to ask for choices or to say 'no' if it feels like a course of action needs to happen for 'the good of the baby'. The moment fear enters, judgement and reason leave the room.

Often parents feel like they did speak up but weren't heard or listened to. Sometimes this is because their care providers were not very caring (perhaps the result of compassion fatigue or of their own trauma and fear). Not being heard, or being ignored usually feels pretty bad for anyone. Feelings of anger and unworthiness are a common result of this treatment. Ultimately being ignored leads to a lack of trust for healthcare professionals and maternity services.

The freeze response

Sometimes, in very stressful situations when fighting or fleeing aren't options, a third strategy is utilised: the freeze response.

The freeze response is activated when we are in a stressful, life threatening situation that we cannot escape from. On the freeze response scale, the two extremes are dissociation and fainting.

Dissociation happens to protect us from what is intolerably stressful, unbearable and life threatening. The mind can literally go somewhere else until it is over, and the body is also inactive, essentially playing dead. From the outside, this can look like a very compliant and willing woman. Dissociation on the one hand makes difficult situations easier to cope with in the moment, as we mentally and physically 'check out'. However, it can also make it easier for abuses to happen since the body doesn't fight back.

The freeze response and dissociation are not a conscious choice. The response stems from our autonomic nervous system in order to save our life when things get too bad. As Dr Stephen Porges, psychiatrist and author of The Polyvagal Theory, has explained:

"Survivors are shamed and blamed because they didn't mobilise, fight and make an effort. That's a misunderstanding. It's a poorly informed explanation because the body goes into that [freeze] state and they can't move. The [Polyvagal] theory had traction because it gave survivors feelings of validation. Survival was really an expression of the heroic nature of our body in trying to save us. Sometimes it goes into a state in which we can't move, but the objective is to raise our pain thresholds and to make us appear to be less viable to the predator."

Anke Velstra, a Dutch birth counsellor who has survived birth trauma and now frequently works with other women seeking to overcome trauma symptoms relating to birth, says:

"Women frequently carry a lot of heavy guilt and shame about what happened during their births. They don't understand why they didn't speak up, why they couldn't say 'no' and so they feel like they were collusive in their own poor treatment during birth. Many women feel that their body failed them. Explaining the polyvagal theory and knowing that it was a survival response, has helped them so much. To know that their body did not fail them, but did the best thing it could do in this awful situation. Knowing this, gives them so much relief. Understanding that it is a survival mechanism within the body that causes this and that actually their natural response to

threat (freezing) saved their life.

Women I have worked with in the past have voiced experiences that described dissociation during birth:

Looking back, there were times during labour, and even afterwards, when I think "Why didn't I tell the midwife what I wanted?" I feel angry with myself for not expressing my needs and desires. But at the time I couldn't see any option other than complete submission. I was so frightened and overwhelmed, I just went with it. Even in the hours after my son was born, I was still terrified that something bad would happen to us if I didn't comply fully with the medical staff's demands. A nurse took him and was bouncing him up and down roughly to stop him crying. It was horrible, but I felt utterly unable to speak up or act. When I think back to that scene, I hate myself for not standing up for my son, for not taking him away from her.
-Saphia

'I think a lot about the birth and can pinpoint the moment of everything going wrong as the moment I got on the bed. The moment I went against instinct and chose medical intervention over the trust in my own body. There was no good reason to wheel me off to theatre, but I don't blame the hospital staff. I blame myself for not speaking up.'
– Lauren

'I just felt like road kill.'
– Ariadna

4. AN ANXIETY TOOLKIT: THE BASICS

Not all of the exercises in this book will appeal to you. However, the most essential exercise is learning relaxation, grounding and mindfulness. Once you learn these skills, they are a resource for life which can always be used to lower your anxiety, tension and stress levels and provide you with the space to rest, repair and recover from your experience.

Breathing exercise
The natural antidote to the fight or flight response described above is a process of relaxation which begins by telling the body that it is time to relax. It then introduces a physical state of relaxation into the body, from where it is possible to mentally relax.

Conscious relaxation always begins with breath work. This is because the way in which we breathe provides the lead for the body's other systems, such as the cardiovascular system, to function in a healthy manner.

Recovering from a traumatic birth – a practical guide

When our breathing is rapid and shallow, it signals to the autonomic nervous system that something is wrong. Unless the excess oxygen created by rapid breathing in the blood is utilised with physical action then it can trigger the body's fight or flight response, even when there is no danger present. This way of breathing can trigger a panic attack.

When we breathe deeply, and more importantly when we breathe out for longer than we breathe in, it tells the autonomic nervous system that it's time for the body to relax. For this reason, a longer outward breath is always the beginning of physical and mental relaxation.

Breathing in this way has three benefits:
1. **It focuses attention in the present moment; when we are in the 'here and now' we do not experience anxiety, which is usually always concerned with a future that hasn't happened.**
2. **It allows the heart to adopt a good resting rhythm.**
3. **It facilitates the delivery of a good amount of oxygen to all the essential muscle groups and organs, ensuring optimum function and wellbeing**

This longer outward breath can be achieved in several ways. One popular way is to begin by sitting with your hands resting just above your stomach and counting the deep inward breath until your ribcage expands. Whatever number you reach for a full breath in, maybe four, five or six, then allow your outward breath to be two or three counts longer. Sometimes it helps to pause at the end of your exhalation before you breath in again to ensure that all the old air has left your lungs before you take you next inhalation. So if you count to four on your inhalation, try and lengthen your outward breath to a six or seven. If you counted to six on the in-breath, then try an eight- or nine-count outward breath. Then pause.

Sometimes people don't like counting, and prefer simply to become aware of the quality of each deep inward breath and each longer outward breath. If you find counting to be a distraction, just notice instead the physical sensations, the temperature of your breath, and the sound of the air as it enters and leaves your body. You can draw your attention to the physical sensation of your ribcage expanding as you breathe deep into your stomach. As you exhale perhaps you can sense your muscles relaxing and your body dropping further down into the surface that is supporting you.

It can be soothing to think of each outward breath as a wave of relaxation. You can achieve this by focusing on the potential of each outward breath to wash away tension from your body and cleanse any worries from your mind.

It really doesn't matter which breathing technique you favour, as long as you are able to use your breathing to redirect your attention away from the thoughts swirling around your mind, and instead focus on your body. This in itself is a calming, grounding action and the beginning of any relaxation process.

After a few relaxation breaths, you can then move your attention to the muscles in your body, one at a time. Starting by focusing on the muscles in your forehead, temples and eyes, giving them permission to soften and loosen. As you focus your attention on these muscles just notice how comfortable they feel as they relax. What else do you notice?

Then take your focus to your cheeks and jaw. Ask these muscles to become limp with relaxation. As you feel these muscles soften and loosen, what else do you notice about this part of your face? Does your jaw drop or recede as you give the muscle permission to let go? Do your teeth part a little? These are signs that the muscles are completely relaxed.

As you breath out now, can you sense that feeling of relaxation drifting downwards over the muscles of your neck and throat? Give these muscles permission to relax even further. As you take your attention to the muscles around your shoulders, can you give them permission to let go of any tension or tightness? Can you feel them fully relax and maybe even drop down, away from your neck, as those muscles release and let go? Next, imagine this feeling of relaxation flowing down through the muscles in your arms, down through to your wrists, your hands, and all the way down to your fingertips. As you focus on these muscles, give them permission to fully relax and let go. Feel them soften and loosen comfortably.

On you next exhalation, imagine your breath as a wave of relaxation washing down through the muscles in your back, as you give them permission to fully relax. As you take your attention to your back, you can begin to imagine that all the muscles here are melting into relaxation. As you feel all the muscles in your back releasing any tension, can you feel yourself sinking even more comfortably into the surface that is supporting you?

With your next exhalation, allow this pleasant wave of relaxation to wash down over all the muscles in your chest and abdomen, easing away any tension and helping you to drift further into comfort. As you begin to notice the muscles in your legs, give permission for your thighs, knees and calves to become comfortably loose and limp with relaxation. You are deep down relaxed now, with a wonderful feeling of comfort radiating down from the very top of your head to the tips of your toes.

You can access your own audio recording of this relaxation here https://traumaticbirthrecovery.com/book-resources/

Recovering from a traumatic birth – a practical guide

It is important for all of us to have the ability to experience relaxation in this way. It is the first tenet of good emotional health and thankfully these relaxation techniques are beginning to be taught as part of the daily routine for some school children. Having a skill that they can call on in times of stress will make a huge difference to the emotional wellbeing of these children throughout their lives.

The World Health Organization advises that adults should get 150 minutes of brisk exercise throughout the week to remain in good physical health. It is my hope that the same recommendation will be made for 10 minutes of mindful relaxation every day. This should be considered as obvious and necessary to good health as the need to eat five portions of fresh fruit and vegetables per day.

When encountering this breathing exercise, maybe you have had one of the following thoughts.

"What's the point? This will never take away the pain I feel."

"I haven't got time to stop and practice something that appears to have no immediate effect."

"How can something so simple help me, when my feelings are so complex?"

"This doesn't work for me. I must be the exception to the rule."

Recovering from a traumatic birth – a practical guide

"I can't do it."

It is completely natural to feel an initial resistance to this kind of breathing and progressive relaxation technique. If any of these statements or thoughts chimes with your experience of practicing breathing and progressive relaxation then please do not worry. Put these thoughts aside for now, and keep practicing the techniques on a daily basis for 10 minutes, without expectation and without judgement. It will work, and one day when you don't do it you will notice the difference!

One of the tricks of an anxious mind is that it wants you to keep thinking, thinking, thinking about your feelings, about the past, about the future. However, it is this constant rumination that contributes to the everyday experience of fear, worry and pain. If you 'think' that relaxation won't work for you, then try to recognise this thought as a symptom of anxiety, which is keeping you stuck in a loop. The only way to begin breaking the cycle of anxiety is to practice relaxation regularly. This way you can develop a mindful relationship with your thoughts that allows you to recognise anxious thinking. Relaxation means turning off the tap of constant thought that is exacerbating your fear and pain. At first it provides temporary relief. Then, with regular practice, it creates a behavioural response that can quickly bring on relaxation each time you connect with your breath or recognise that you have been having anxious thoughts.

Recovering from a traumatic birth – a practical guide

Each time you practice the breathing technique, you will notice that you can relax more quickly and easily than the last time. You will also notice that this focused attention on your physical sensations quietens your mind, slows down and eventually stops the flow of thought. Even if this only happens for a few minutes as you practice the relaxation technique, your mind will get a well-needed rest from constant fearful, anxious and worrisome thinking. Please do not underestimate the benefit of turning down the constant machinations of your conscious thought, even if only for a short time every day.

Once you begin to enjoy this break from anxious thinking, and you are feeling the benefits of deep and comfortable relaxation, then you can choose to extend your holiday from anxious thoughts.

Go to the resources section of the website: https://traumaticbirthrecovery.com/book-resources/ to listen to a guided visualisation that allows you to use your imagination to create an even greater sensation of peace and ease. Listening to this regularly will help you to benefit from a feeling of wellness, renewal and healing throughout your body and mind.

Grounding technique

If your symptoms include feelings of panic, then it is helpful to learn a 'grounding technique' that you can access quickly before panic overwhelms you. Grounding techniques allow you to instantly drop out of the fight or flight response. Rather than being tipped into frightening feelings of panic, dread or loss of control, a grounding technique can bring you back into the present moment, allowing you to reassure yourself (and your amygdala) that there is no danger present.

Panic feels horrible. It can include feelings of complete loss of control and dread, as well as a racing heart, sweating, and problems with digestion. It is therefore easy to begin to fear this experience. If you reach this stage of 'fearing the fear', they you can be vulnerable to experiencing regular panic attacks.

Knowledge and experience of a grounding technique can prevent panic becoming a regular experience and help you to regain control.

There are hundreds of different ways of grounding. The key is finding something that appeals to you and which you can practice frequently, ideally after using a relaxation technique and before panic is even present. Pairing a grounding technique with listening to a relaxation session creates a link between the two sensations, which will eventually allow you to automatically achieve deep relaxation via the grounding technique alone. This is usually quicker and easier than a full 10-minute relaxation session.

Popular grounding techniques include:

Recovering from a traumatic birth – a practical guide

Going outside in bare feet, and standing on earth or grass. While doing this, focus on the sensation of the ground beneath your feet. You might like to feel the ground with your hands too. Notice the colour of the ground or grass, its temperature and texture, and how it feels against your skin. Then begin to breathe deeply into your stomach and exhale slowly, all the way out. At the end of your breath, pause momentarily before you inhale again.

Running your hands under warm or cold water. Focus on the sensations in your hands. Do they change colour? How cold can you tolerate the water to be? While doing this, use the relaxation breathing technique mentioned earlier in this chapter (deep diaphragmatic breath in, longer breath out).

Using a weighted blanket. This can lower your level of arousal and help you to come back into the present moment. Focus on how the blanket feels, its softness, its heaviness, its smell, and any other sensations. While doing this, use the relaxation breathing technique as you continue to notice all the sensations of the blanket.

Stroking a pet is a great way of lowering arousal and tipping the autonomic nervous system into a parasympathetic (relaxation) response. It is for this reason that airplane passengers in the USA may be permitted to travel with an 'emotional support animal' to help them to self-soothe if they are afraid of flying.

Recovering from a traumatic birth – a practical guide

It is important to find a grounding technique that works for you. The key ingredient for any grounding technique is that it should make you notice what is going on right now around you, with all your senses. This literally grounds you back in the present moment. It brings you out of your head (where fear and panic are rampant) This action effectively turns off the fight or flight part of the brain (the amygdala).

One key consideration in choosing a grounding technique is its accessibility. So, if you find that panic attacks take place while you are at home, then any of the above techniques may work for you. However, very often panic can come on suddenly without warning and outside of the home.

I'm going to introduce you to a grounding technique that you can use anywhere, and which I and others refer to as the 5-4-3-2-1 technique. The 5-4-3-2-1 technique simply asks you to name five things that you can see, four things you can touch, three things that you can hear, two things you can smell and one thing that you can taste. Sometimes it helps to say these things out loud. Again, focus on your breathing while doing this technique, ensuring that your outward breath is longer than your inward breath.

This technique has several advantages:

1. It can be used absolutely anywhere

Recovering from a traumatic birth – a practical guide

2. It engages all the senses and so has wide appeal
3. It is always available
4. It takes the amygdala offline as it calls into action the prefrontal cortex of the brain.

Once you feel that you are able to use these relaxation, visualisation and grounding techniques to reduce distress, then you may feel ready to examine your traumatic experiences and begin the process of understanding why they are hurting you.

5. UNPACKING WHAT HAPPENED, HOW YOU FELT THEN, AND HOW IT FEELS NOW: AN EXERCISE TO BRING CLARITY AND UNDERSTANDING

It is not always necessary with other kinds of trauma to investigate precisely what happened and how that made a person feel. For example, if you are attacked by a stranger in the street, then this is an illegal act punishable by law, and it is generally accepted that this will be a traumatic event with strong emotions attached. However, with birth and perinatal trauma, women are often so confused by their experience and the resulting feelings that there is value in examining it in some detail. Compared to other transgressions, such as being the victim of an illegal street attack, perinatal trauma generally occurs against a legal, institutional backdrop, where the acts were carried out 'for the health and safety of the baby'. This can be confusing and may cause a great deal of anger, since we still feel wronged at a human level despite the legality and 'moral purpose' of the act.

Recovering from a traumatic birth – a practical guide

Sometimes these violating and transgressing protocols can be re-triggering of previous traumas. Conservative estimates say that one in five women are survivors of sexual abuse and, for these women, clumsy maternity protocols and bad care can easily re-trigger traumatic memories. Regardless of past experiences, vaginal examinations can be potentially distressing for any woman since we are encouraged to think of our vaginas as private and sacrosanct areas of our bodies. For survivors of sexual abuse, a vaginal examination therefore has the potential to be a particularly stressful and re-triggering experience. Many women find that vaginal examinations re-trigger old traumas without necessarily understanding why. This can be as simple as the body responding in panic as the same body parts are manipulated by a relative stranger.

Directly after giving birth, there is rarely the time or space to process our experience in a way that illuminates why we feel the way we do. Emotions can simply feel raw, rather than being attributable to any particular thing. I believe there is huge value in understanding not only how you feel about what has happened, but also in confronting how it affects your thoughts, feelings and ways of responding now. Understanding the day-to-day impact of these thoughts, feelings and responses is a good starting point, as you begin to unpick the effect that birth trauma is having on your life now.

Recovering from a traumatic birth – a practical guide

Unpacking exercise

This unpacking worksheet, available as a download at this link https://traumaticbirthrecovery.com/book-resources/ encourages you to work through the traumatic event by detailing what happened and how that made you feel at the time. The last column also asks you to consider the ways in which the experience continues to affect you today. You can consider how it impacts on your thoughts and feelings, but also the ways in which you respond to these thoughts and feelings.

Here are a few examples of what a typical worksheet might look like in different scenarios.

As you do this exercise, it is really important to acknowledge in an open and honest manner the ways in which your past experience continues to affect your daily life now. Unfortunately, we cannot change what happened in our past. However, we can change how we feel presently. It is important to understand that this isn't about 'reframing' heavy feelings or 'looking on the bright side'. You have an absolute right to feel the way that you do, given what you have experienced. This exercise is about understanding your current feelings as a way of moving them, softening them or even lifting them so that you have the space to feel something else, something that serves you better.

Recovering from a traumatic birth – a practical guide

As you work through this exercise, consider how your past experience continues to affect your relationship with your partner and your child(ren), as well as other relationships and friendships. Consider how the trauma symptoms affect your day-to-day life. Are there tasks or activities that you are avoiding? Have you begun to adopt negative coping mechanisms to manage your symptoms? Does your past experience currently have an impact on your sense of self? Has it affected your confidence? How do you think about yourself as a mother? Has it left you with a heavy sense of guilt or shame? Do you find yourself going to lengths to conceal or make up for these feelings? Does what happened in the past affect your hopes for the future?

It might be that only some of these issues apply to you. However, I urge you to be gentle with yourself as you confront these questions. This is difficult, gut-wrenching stuff to think about, and you need to be kind to yourself. Examining the pain caused by your experience, both to you and perhaps also to your loved ones, takes a lot of bravery and courage. Yet it is the only way to fully recover. Evaluating the ways in which you are still affected by the trauma you experienced will help you reach a clear recognition and acknowledgement of the impact on your current life, and is the only way to move forward.

Your experience is unique to you. However, it is very common to find this part of the exercise difficult and upsetting. I encourage you to go as slowly as feels right and, when you are ready, to share your experience and find support on the closed Facebook community of parents all travelling the same road to recovery. Be kind to yourself as you complete this exercise. Explain to those close to you that they may need to be extra gentle with you, and tell them what you need in terms of their understanding and support.

If this exercise seems too mechanical or dissecting, you may instead prefer to write about your experience. Keeping a journal about what happened and how it continues to show up in your life can have an equally cathartic effect. Once you have put these experiences, thoughts and feelings down on paper, you can begin to place some distance between what happened in the past and how you feel now. Either exercise can be useful if you later want to discuss your experience with your care providers or if you are keen to plan for a better birth next time.

During either of these exercises, we need to mindful that any re-telling or remembering has the potential to be very distressing and retraumatising, strengthening the neural pathways that we eventually want to break. You should only progress to this stage when you feel assured that you have the relaxation skills that you will need to reinstate feelings of calm and ease following the exercise.

6. GETTING ACKNOWLEDGEMENT AND VALIDATION OF YOUR TRAUMATIC EXPERIENCE

I believe that one of the most important steps towards feeling better and recovering your old sense of self is in having your story heard and acknowledged and your feelings validated. There are several ways that you can do this:

- On the closed Facebook group for people who are also using this process to feel better. You can find the details here https://traumaticbirthrecovery.com/book-resources/

- At a formal debriefing service provided by the hospital, which I would only recommend if they are able to guarantee that the person conducting the debrief has specialist trauma-informed training.

- By using the directory of trained birth professionals here

Recovering from a traumatic birth – a practical guide

> https://traumaticbirthrecovery.com/online-courses-for-professionals/ here you can find somebody you can talk to about your experience (many of these birth professionals deliver other services that you might also find useful, such as doulaing, midwifery, yoga, massage and more).

Ideally, any listening or debriefing service should hear your story without judgement, comment or interruption. It should simply be an opportunity for your story to be heard by external ears one last time, as we know that constant re-telling is potentially re-traumatising. Receiving acknowledgement of your experience and validation of your feelings has huge potential for helping you to heal and recover.

Unfortunately, good listening often doesn't happen when we share our difficult stories with others and can, when done badly, be re-traumatising. In the case of birth trauma, friends, family and maternity services alike often feel uncomfortable just hearing your story and how it made you feel. They may try to rush in and 'justify', 'rationalise' or 'fix' what occurred. This leaves the storyteller feeling unreasonable, unbelieved and irrational, which is the opposite of an opportunity to heal and find peace through being heard. For this reason, I would only advise sharing your story with others if you are sure that they are trained in how to listen without judgement. If you request a hospital debrief or listening service then be clear about what YOU want from it. Because it should be

Recovering from a traumatic birth – a practical guide

a chance for you to feel better, not a chance for the care provider to make excuses for poor care or a crappy policy. Setting an agenda for this meeting can give the care provider a heads up, while helping to give you the confidence to stay on track and have your needs met during the discussion.

Things you might want to include in the agenda are:

- Your desire to have your story heard, the pain caused from your experience acknowledged, and your feelings validated.
- Your desire for the midwife involved in your care to have your experience fed back to him or her.
- Your desire to have health care professionals understand how your experience of their care made you feel.
- Your desire to understand why certain things happened.
- Your desire to gain clarity about *what* happened.
- Your desire to hear an apology (even if there is no liability).
- Your desire to receive assurances that what happened to you won't happen again, either to you or to other women.

One of the major benefits of having your experience 'officially heard' by someone (preferably someone trained in trauma informed listening) is that it can provide some

Recovering from a traumatic birth – a practical guide

closure and for many people it signals their readiness to move towards feeling differently day to day.

If you don't want to meet face-to-face with someone to have your story heard, try writing your story down, including how it has impacted on you, and posting or emailing it instead. This can also have therapeutic benefit. Remember to include what you would like the receiver to do as a result of your letter, if indeed you want them to acknowledge receipt of it. Do you want an apology? Acknowledgement of your pain or suffering? A change in policy? Guarantees that it won't happen again to you or anyone else? Ask for what you need, even if it is not given, you will feel better for being clear about your needs.

You have a few options when it comes to addressing your letter, and this list isn't inclusive of everyone you might consider:

- Head of Midwifery of the maternity unit where you gave birth
- The NHS Patient Advice and Liaison Service (PALS)
- Your local Care Quality Commission (CQC) search online for your local contact details
- Maternity Voice Partnership (MVP). Most maternity services have an MVP group of 'service

Recovering from a traumatic birth – a practical guide

users' which sends feedback to midwives on their service.

7. HOW WOULD YOU LIKE THINGS TO BE DIFFERENT, IF YOU COULD CHOOSE? USING A SOLUTION-FOCUSED APPROACH

If you have been practicing the relaxation and visualisation exercises regularly and are beginning to feel their positive effects then you will be ready for the next exercise.

When we are gripped by trauma symptoms, it can feel like we are at the mercy of those symptoms. As we saw above, it is a natural response for the brain to re-trigger the fight or flight response whenever a stimulus is present, even if it is only remembered or imagined. On the other hand, imagining a different future can begin to lay down new neural pathways. This happens as we begin to rehearse different way of thinking, feeling and responding, day-to-day.

This might sound strange, since it means using your imagination to go against what you have been experiencing. You may well feel that this seems like an impossible or even inappropriate task, but being able to use your imagination to create different ways of feeling about the past is key to changing those feelings, thoughts and ways of responding.

Unfortunately, nothing can change what happened to you. However, you do have an opportunity to break the ties that bind you to that past event. You can sever the connections to the past in a way that allows you to remember what happened, but in a way that does not hurt you anymore.

Take a look at the last exercise, where you wrote down the ways in which your past experience continues to affect you. Now, when you look at these impacts on your current life, imagine what your life would be like if those symptoms, feelings and ways of responding were gone.

This future may well feel out of your reach because of the heavy feelings that you are currently experiencing. But take a moment to imagine what the opposite of this experience would be like.

When we are consumed with weighty, painful emotions like anger, guilt, shame, fear or sadness, it is really common to think 'well, I would just stop feeling anger, guilt, shame, fear or sadness'. However this exercise asks you to consider what the opposite of that would actually be like. So, what would it feel like to be free of anger? What would the opposite of feeling fearful be? What would it be like to be free of guilt? Or shame? So rather than thinking 'I would not have the negative emotion', try imagining the positive opposite of that emotion instead.

This exercise takes patience and a bit of perseverance, because when we are gripped by our problem we tend to fixate and ruminate on what that problem is. This, ironically, just brings us more of the problem. So we might think 'I wish I didn't feel so anxious about getting pregnant again', but thinking this only encourages more anxiety. What is needed is an experience of what the solution would be. To imagine with curiosity what it would feel like to *not* be anxious when thinking about getting pregnant again. So, for example, if we imagine that the opposite of anxiety might be feeling peaceful. So then you could consider: 'If I felt peaceful about getting pregnant again, what else would change?' How would your partner know that you were feeling more peaceful about becoming pregnant again? What else would they notice about you if you were feeling more peaceful? What would your child or children notice about you if you were feeling more peaceful? How would feeling more peaceful influence the way that you think about yourself? If you felt more peaceful about the thought of being pregnant again, what would you be doing differently day to day? You can begin to create the solution state by imagining what it would feel like.

Of course, imagining the changes that you would like to experience are not always enough for the change to actually occur, but they are the start of change.

Recovering from a traumatic birth – a practical guide

When doing this exercise, be mindful of using critical thought or judgement that has a tendency to chime in 'but you can't do that, feel that, have that'. Just allow your imagination to run free and create your solution state for you. Keep asking 'if X changed, what else would be different?'

Write down your answers, or draw them if you are artistically inclined. Try to consider all aspects of your life in your solution-focused approach to feeling differently.

Use the relaxation exercise to experience a future where these changes have already taken place.

Here are some examples of what this might look like:

Lilia had a difficult birth nearly three years ago but recovered well. However, her partner now wants to have another child and Lilia has found herself consumed with anxiety, anger and fear when she thinks about pregnancy and birth. It is causing many arguments between them both. Lilia feels that her partner doesn't understand how difficult their daughter's birth was for her. She is angry at his lack of understanding and what she feels is his lack of love or concern for her. She would like to feel less angry at her partner and less afraid of pregnancy and birth. Lilia isn't sure whether she actually *wants* to be pregnant again, even if she didn't feel afraid. However, she doesn't want fear to be the deciding factor in their future. In thinking about what would change if she was less angry, Lilia decides that she would like to feel calmer when the subject of having more children is raised. She would be able to discuss it neutrally, like any other future plans. If she felt calmer when discussing it, then her husband would notice that she was more relaxed at home generally. If she felt calmer she would be able to show affection again and be more relaxed in his company. Ultimately, she decides that if she were calmer, she would be able to make up her own mind about having more children, based on her own and her family's desires, free of fear and anger.

Becky had two traumatic births where she felt that she had been treated badly by the maternity services. Despite feeling that she had been treated cruelly by her care providers, and therefore feeling justifiably angry, she also felt guilty about the violent beginning to her children's lives and wondered whether she could have acted differently to bring about a different outcome for them. This doubt seeded an anxiety about her children's health, which became very pronounced when one child experienced delayed developmental milestones. The anxiety and guilt became an everyday feature of family life, tainting their parenting experience. For Becky, this was weighted with guilt and anger about her past birth experiences and a constant anxiety about what the future held for her child's ability to thrive in the world. When she tried to imagine her life without these feelings, she thought that she would physically feel lighter, that she would have more time and energy to experience joy with her family, but also that she would be able to feel more accepting of her child's unique beauty, humour and chattiness. She would even be able to feel proud of her child's uniqueness. If all of these things changed, she conceded that her relationship could also change too. She believed that she could begin to reclaim some of her old, fun-loving self again.

It is normal for some folk to experience resistance to a solution-focused approach. After all, we are used to living with a medicalised view of treating symptoms, often pharmacologically, rather than looking at the problem from the inside out and considering the person's whole experience of it. However, it is incredibly effective for creating lasting change when we are able to get in the habit of using it.

We create our own experience through the thoughts we have and the feelings that they generate, so we need to begin to be mindful of what those thoughts and feelings are. When they create a sense of fear about the future or an ever-present feeling of unease, then we can use a solution-focused approach to ask ourselves 'what would it be like without this feeling?' And then, 'if that were so, what else in my life would change?'

The more we focus on the pain of our trauma, the more pain is generated. Knowing our problem really well just multiplies the problem, when instead we need to begin rehearsing and experiencing how the solution feels.

This might feel tricky if you are feeling a lot of anger or blame towards someone. This exercise isn't about absolving them of their part in your trauma, but simply allowing you to consider the changes that would occur if that blame or anger was lifted.

If you do still feel overwhelming feelings of anger and blame, then having your story heard and your feelings validated (Chapter 6) may help pave the way for you to consider a future without these feelings.

Notice how the idea of this exercise is not to reframe what happened by implying that no one was at fault, for example, or placing new meaning on what happened to you. The purpose of the exercise is simply to move away from the pain of what happened by considering how you would like to experience life without the weight of trauma symptoms dragging you down.

8. BREAKING THE PATTERNS AND MAKING SPACE FOR NEW WAYS OF THINKING, FEELING AND RESPONDING

In Chapter 3 we talked about the neurobiological process whereby the feelings that remain after a difficult perinatal event are constantly re-triggered, causing heavy feelings to flood back each time. In this chapter, we will discover exercises that can break the links in the brain that are continually being re-triggered. With these links (neural pathways) broken, there is a window of opportunity to experience different ways of thinking, feeling and responding to the cues that were previously triggering painful feelings.

Hopefully, the previous exercise involving a solution-focused approach has provided you with a vision or goal for your future, which you can experience in the place of the trauma symptoms and feelings.

Rewind exercise

There are several exercises for breaking the patterns of trauma within the brain. The first is the Rewind exercise.

Recovering from a traumatic birth – a practical guide

This exercise must only be used if you feel confident that you are able to relax and ground yourself in the present, should the memories of your experience become upsetting. If you are uncertain about using this exercise on your own then please consider working with a trained practitioner who will be able to guide you. You can find a directory of Traumatic Birth Recovery trained practitioners here: www.traumaticbirthrecovery.com/practitioners

Before you begin the Rewind exercise, take a moment to score how upsetting you find the memory of the difficult or traumatic event. Score using a scale of one to 10, where one is feeling completely calm when you remember what happened, and 10 is feeling extremely upset when you remember what happened.

The first stage is to focus on your breathing in exactly the same way that you have been practicing in the earlier relaxation exercises. You will want to feel confident in your ability to use your breath throughout to ground you back in the present moment, if necessary. Then the audio recording will guide you through the physical relaxation, again as you have been used to experiencing with the other audio recordings. You will then be encouraged to create your place of relaxation using all of your senses. While you are here, the audio will guide you to visualise a screen. On this screen, you will be encouraged to watch the memory of your event from beginning to end, starting

Recovering from a traumatic birth – a practical guide

at a point just before the event began, and ending at the point when you finally felt safe again.

When your memory has ended, you will see yourself in your mind's eye pressing a 'rewind' button and watching the memory move backwards, at high speed, all the way back to the beginning.

You will be guided to watch and rewind your memory three times, but each time the visualisation will be slightly different.

The first time it will be suggested that you can float out of your body and drift a few feet backwards so that effect is that you are able to watch yourself, watching the memory on the screen in front of you.

The second time it will be suggested that you can simply watch your memory on the screen in front of you and then rewind it back to the beginning when it reaches the end.

The final time it will be suggested that you can float up into the screen and experience the memory as if you were in it this time (so no longer watching it from a distance). This time you experience the memory from beginning to end and then rewind it back to the beginning.

Although it will be suggested that you view your memory in these slightly different ways each time, it is very common for people to report that they struggle to watch it differently each time. If this happens to you, don't worry just allow yourself to experience it in whichever way feels right for you. The important thing is to play it from start to finish and then rewind it back to the beginning.

Because of the relaxation that precedes the Rewind exercise, visualising the event again shouldn't promote upset or retraumatising feelings, although it is understandable if a tear or two is shed. If you begin to feel unsafe or out of control at any point, then discontinue the exercise and focus your attention on grounding yourself back into the present moment. Open your eyes and name five things you can see, four things you can touch, three things you can hear, two things you can smell and one thing you can taste. Focus on your breathing by inhaling deep into your stomach and exhaling all of the old air. Pause for a moment at the end of you outward breath before you breath in again. Breathe like this for a while and begin to notice the seat you are sitting in and your feet making contact with the ground.

You can share your experience of using this process and the other exercises in the closed Facebook group, and read how others have experienced the exercises.

Continue to practice relaxation on a daily basis, including your solution-focused state at the end of each relaxation.

Recovering from a traumatic birth – a practical guide

See yourself in the near future with the feelings, thoughts and ways of responding in place. Notice all of the changes that have occurred in your life as a result of those old painful, anxious ways being lifted.

'Alex helped me to use the Rewind technique in the weeks leading up to the birth, to help me overcome past traumatic memories that were causing me anxiety about medical intervention. I visualised myself in a calming place that I remembered from childhood, and spent a few minutes every day going through the Rewind exercise after first doing a calming, grounding exercise. In doing so I found myself able to make better sense of the traumatic experiences I'd had in the past, and view them in a new light that didn't cause me distress. It didn't completely dissipate my fears about going into hospital, but it did make birth feel more manageable, meaning that I had a more relaxed and confident pregnancy.' - Saphia

Letting go – Lauren's story

"As a result of the complications from my traumatic birth, I developed post-natal depression in the first week of Ellen's life. Ellen had developed colic by this point also, which didn't help the bonding process. We recognised it early on and I received counselling within a CBT [cognitive behavioural therapy] group run by the NHS. This helped in as much as getting me out of the house and meeting other mums who were struggling. Gradually I began to pick myself up, but I was far from being happy. I felt a little like I was going through the motions, getting through each day. At the time I was grateful for just being able to do that. I obsessed over the birth

Recovering from a traumatic birth – a practical guide

and would think about it constantly. What I could have done differently, what the midwives could have done differently, etc. I finally got around to sending Alex my birth story in August, eight months after the event. She suggested I come to see her for a session. At the time I thought I might as well, it couldn't hurt, but didn't fully believe I needed to. How wrong I was! We started the session with talking over the events of the birth and the time that followed. I gradually let my guard down and started to realise that it was far from a resolved issue. Alex asked astute questions that I think nobody had dared to ask me, and I hadn't dared to ask myself. I had a lot of pent-up guilt over the whole situation, and a lot of anger. It also became clear that a lot of my feelings towards it were damaging my relationship not only with my daughter, but with my husband too. I had a very poor attitude towards myself, and blamed myself for a lot of things that were beyond my control.

As I entered a deep state of relaxation, the emotions I had locked away came to the surface. It shocked me that I had buried all of this so deeply. I was finally honest with myself. Alex talked me through letting go of all the negativity, playing it through in my mind a few times and then destroying it. Discarding it.

I walked away a lighter person. How corny it sounds but the sun was shining and the birds were singing. I sat in the car before driving away, took a deep breath, and felt a huge sense of relief. I was free of despair! It was something I had learned to live with, not realising I didn't have to live with it at all.

I would say that day was the turning point in my new career as a mother. I have found the joy that it brings, and oh my – what joy! I no longer 'go through the motions' of motherhood. I am savouring each day, and above all, can't wait to add to my nest and do it all again! I can highly recommend birth trauma treatment. Birth isn't

Recovering from a traumatic birth – a practical guide

always beautiful; it can be a hugely traumatic thing. I was so ashamed to admit that it had affected me so much. It still seems to be such a taboo subject. I'm so glad I opened up about it, and so grateful to Alex for helping me to let go."

Using EFT to dissipate unhelpful patterns and feelings
EFT stands for Emotional Freedom Technique. It has been in existence for a long time but was most recently developed by Gary Craig. It is completely safe, gentle and easy to use.

EFT works to clear the energetic disruption that can occur when heavy and toxic feelings remain following a difficult or traumatic event. Acupuncturists have long used their knowledge of the Chinese meridian lines that run through our bodies to cure ailments. EFT utilises this same system to release blocked energy fields and bring relief.

This is done by gentle tapping on certain points around the hand, face, torso and head while first affirming the feelings that are getting you down, and then gradually replacing them with new feelings, thoughts or ways of being that you wish to experience.

You can use tapping when you feel overwhelmed by the emotions that you are experiencing. Before you begin tapping, identify the emotion and name it, for example fear or sadness or anger. Then score the strength of this feeling using a scale from zero to 10, where zero is very calm and relaxed and 10 is very distressed.

Look at the diagram below and tap using two fingers firmly on each point as you affirm the following sentence:

"Even though I have these feelings of [name the feelings here], I completely love and accept myself."

You should tap for a few moments (for example, eight taps) on each point as you continually say over and over:

"Even though I have these feelings of [name the feelings here], I completely love and accept myself."

Complete one whole round of tapping and then re-score. How does it feel now on a scale of zero to 10? Keep tapping and re-scoring each round. As the score comes down, change the words to:

"Even though I have these feelings of [name the feeling] I know how to be [use a feeling from your solution-focused work, such as calm, peaceful, present, joyful or happy]."

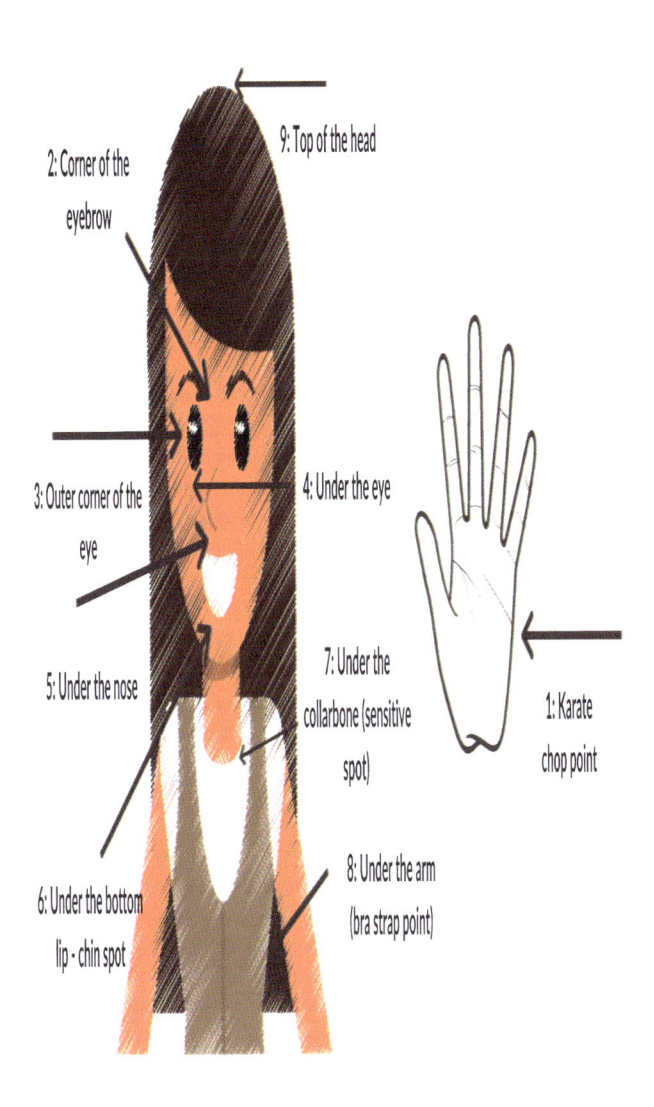

Recovering from a traumatic birth – a practical guide

9: Top of the head
2: Corner of the eyebrow
3: Outer corner of the eye
4: Under the eye
5: Under the nose
7: Under the collarbone (sensitive spot)
1: Karate chop point
6: Under the bottom lip - chin spot
8: Under the arm (bra strap point)

Recovering from a traumatic birth – a practical guide

You can use this tapping technique at any time to ground yourself and to allow in the feelings that you wish to experience.

You can access a video demonstration of these techniques here at the resources section
https://traumaticbirthrecovery.com/book-resources/

Self-compassion

Self-compassion can be a powerful practice for parents to adopt, especially for those of us who are prone to relentless self-criticism, self-judgement and rumination of past 'mistakes'.

Self-compassion can release us from so much of the inner torment caused by the high standards that we set for ourselves.

Society and its systems of education and work often praise competition, achievement and attainment of goals. It is what Western capitalism is based on after all; individual pursuit of growth in all its many forms. 'Doing well' is the name of the game and often the praise, acceptance and love we receive is conditionally metered out depending on our 'success' in any given area of life; education, work, relationships, marriage, and so on. We work hard and achieve at school and are rewarded. At work, we strive for promotion and are rewarded. Often this process of striving and achieving is accomplished by a continual process of internal and external evaluation and assessment: 'this is what you did well, this what you need to do better'.

Many of us are trained from a very early age to adopt this habit of constantly measuring and evaluating our efforts. Unfortunately, this habit is a way of being that we can take with us into our parenting experience too, causing multiple problems. Firstly, in the early days of parenting, there is no one around to say 'well done on a good job' or 'you are doing the right thing there, so congratulations and have a pay rise'. Even when babies eat and sleep well, it can still feel hard and there is no immediate reward or pay off for this gruelling work. You won't even get the weekend off! If your baby has additional needs, for example because of difficulties with feeding or sleeping, or if you are recovering from a traumatic birth or postnatal experience, you may feel as though you are losing at parenting. This is especially true if you have brought self-evaluation habits with you into parenthood. Yet, parenting isn't about attainment in the same way that work and education are. Parenting is about the relationship you have with yourself and with your family.

Added to this fairly standard Western cultural habit of constant evaluation, judgement and critique, we also each have an inherent negative bias. Researchers have found that we naturally tend to focus and ruminate on negative stimuli rather than positive stimuli. The theory behind this phenomenon, according to psychologists, is that we have evolved to have a greater perception of negativity and problems in order protect ourselves from danger. We have a tendency to remember difficult events more readily, to think the worst of a situation or of other people, and to perceive our surroundings negatively too. The negative bias increases when we are anxious.

When we become parents, habits of the inner critic and our natural negative bias can collude with the challenging experience of birth and caring for an infant to make us utterly miserable and depressed.

Maybe having a strong inner critic in the past has served you. Perhaps you attribute academic or career success to this ruthless ability to see error and room for improvement in your work. However, this punitive voice that constantly finds fault can morph from 'productive' in the workplace to oppressive in the family space. Relentless judgement can come thick and fast when we become parents because it is, for many of us, a tough and challenging situation filled with lots of steep learning that we have never encountered before.

Our negative bias unhelpfully draws our attention to everything that is wrong – an awful birth experience, challenging feeding, lack of sleep – and then our inner critic weighs in with the 'should try harder', 'needs to do better', 'you're no good at this' inner dialogue, icing our cake of misery.

Recovering from a traumatic birth – a practical guide

It's very common for parents to draw conclusions such as 'I'm not cut out for this', 'I'm a failure', or 'I'm a useless mother/father' and for the full weight of shame to rest upon their already weary shoulders.

This continual self-blame, shame and guilt cycle really undermines our ability to care for ourselves in order to then care for our family. It can grind parents down into depression as negative rumination dominates our world.

<u>Psychology professor and author of the book Self-Compassion,</u> stop beating yourself up and leave insecurity behind, Kristin Neff, shares three core components of self-compassion that I wish were taught to all women about to become mothers. I believe then an understanding of these components would go a long way to protecting new mothers from postnatal depression.

These three core components of self-compassion are: mindfulness (the ability to recognise and observe our harsh inner critic and negative bias), kindness, and humanity (recognition of our connectedness and of our fallibility).

When we begin to see ourselves through the lens of self-compassion we are, in fact, parenting ourselves. We are accessing the inner guide which exists in all of us to support ourselves in a way that allows us to access our own intuition. This is vital when it comes to parenting for the first time.

When the noisy inner critic is subdued by the acknowledgment that we are all human, often trying to do our best in a difficult situation, the judgement and admonishment that often accompanies it just melts away.

Kristin Neff explains that, from this vantage point, we create space to choose something better for ourselves, which very often has a positive benefit for our babies and children too:

"Unlike self-criticism, which asks if we are good enough, self-compassion asks 'what's good for you?'"

If you have been blaming yourself for your birth or parenting experience, if your inner critic has been evaluating your 'performance' and making you feel that you are not good enough, then gently noticing this inner dialogue can be the first step towards turning it around.

Be firm in the knowledge that this critiquing is definitely not serving you or helping you to become a better parent.

Acknowledge that your experience, like that of many other parents, is bloody tough. Rather than feel pity in this acknowledgement, focus on the humanity of it. Like so many other parents, you are struggling, learning and making mistakes. Feel that connection with other parents,

Recovering from a traumatic birth – a practical guide

and with it, the humanity of your experience. Allow yourself to feel the pain of your experience, knowing that it makes you human. You don't have to fear what you feel because there is no shame in being human.

Be kind to yourself. Hug yourself. Ask your partner for a hug. Hug your baby. Touch is the biggest act of kindness that we can give or receive. Affirm often and with kindness: 'I am doing the best I can. This is tough but I will get through this hard time'. Keep on asking for the support that you need and don't see this as a sign of weakness but of strength. The right support with breastfeeding, sleeping or subsequent births can make a huge difference to your experience and it is a strength to recognise when you need help and to ask for it. You're not supposed to know everything about parenting or caring for infants. This stuff isn't taught in schools; it is learnt on the job. So surround yourself by loving, kind people who can support you.

'My greatest difficulty is that I think I should be perfect, and that everything should be perfect all the time, and that if it's not perfect, it's no good. I think [bringing self compassion to myself] would make every experience in life, even the really horrible ones, much kinder and softer. I would feel safe.' -Marie

Recovering from a traumatic birth – a practical guide

Feeling better moving forward

Nobody makes a linear recovery from perinatal trauma or its residual symptoms. Your ability to feel better, cope with symptoms and learn strategies to feel differently all depend on other life factors.

Often, parents report that they feel better after a round of therapy or self-care, only to be hit by something else and find that trauma symptoms are re-triggered.

We all experience good and bad days in life. What seems to make us more resilient to the bad days is regular practice of self-care and self-compassion. A regular practice of caring for yourself is a huge act of kindness and can put you back in ownership of your feelings, rather than your feelings owning you. This can have a positive impact on your responses to life's slings and arrows.

Self-care will mean different things to different people. For me, self-care feels good, it calms and centres me, and it restores me back to my true, peaceful nature. This is a true peaceful nature that I believe we all share. For a long time I had no means of self-care. Instead, I relied on alcohol and drugs to cope with what I thought were unbearable and intolerable feelings. These feelings turned out to be anxiety.

Recovering from a traumatic birth – a practical guide

Self-care can include massage, yoga, exercise, walking in nature, spending time with folk who are nurturing and supportive, doing a hobby that immerses your attention and brings joy, getting adequate sleep and rest, and eating nourishing and wholesome foods. Self-care can also include practicing journal-writing and meditation, both of which can support a deeper knowledge of one's self and help you to develop self-compassion, which is key to fostering emotional flexibility and resilience.

Self-care should also include the ability to acknowledge and name unpleasant feelings when we experience them repeatedly. Knowing our feelings, and being able to observe them and accept them, will ultimately bring us peace. When we are intolerant or unaccepting of our heavy emotions, then they become 'sticky'. The practice of observing feelings and accepting them allows these feelings to become fluid.

The experience of parenting can be fraught with anxiety. You may find that anxiety from your own experience of childhood is re-triggered at this time.

Becoming aware of these triggers is the first step to disarming them. Journal-writing and meditation can help in the process of becoming aware of triggers, anxiety and stress.

Try keeping a journal about your fears. Be honest about the triggers and the origins of your fears. Write down some of the beliefs that underpin those anxieties and document how that shows up in your life.

Here is an example from Michelle's journal:

'I feel terrible and so ashamed for screaming at Libby for the mess she has made in her room. She is only four, for goodness sakes, her little face crumpled in shame as I tore shreds off her for not looking after her possessions. Saying she didn't deserve anything nice because she doesn't know how to care for things. Now I realise, looking back, that when I saw her room full of possessions but upside down and messy, that it reminded me of my own childhood when I had nothing, no possessions but living in chaos the whole time. It triggered a feeling of deep shame which quickly turned to anger directed at poor Libby. It's as if I was thinking 'how dare she take all of this for granted? I had nothing when I was her age'. So I shouted at her and now I feel shame again for being jealous of my own daughter. I will talk to her and apologise for losing my temper. I choose to forgive myself and try harder to respond differently next time. I am going to tap on the feeling of shame and see if I can reduce it now.'

Some of the exercises and suggestions in this book might seem to take up too much time, or maybe they feel self-indulgent. I completely understand, because I too used to feel this way about self-care. However, I can honestly say that the time I have invested in knowing myself in a kind and compassionate way has not only been great for my emotional health, but I also enjoy more connected relationships with my family as a result. It really is the key to freedom from anxiety and depression.

9. PLANNING FOR A BETTER BIRTH NEXT TIME

Are you pregnant again, or planning to be? Maybe you recovered well from your last birth experience but anxious feelings are beginning to emerge now that the prospect of having to 'do it again' is on the horizon.

Maybe it's still early days, or you or your partner have vowed 'never again', but you are curious to see what this chapter has to offer.

The good news is that you can have a positive, healing birth experience after a difficult or traumatic one. The bad news is that you may naturally be beginning to feel anxious already, and you may also be experiencing other unpleasant emotions or symptoms as a result of your situation.

Traumatic Birth Recovery

Hopefully you have been able to use the exercises in this book to reduce your anxiety. If you haven't, or if you have found this book late in your pregnancy and feel like you are short on time, then I recommend visiting a birth

Recovering from a traumatic birth – a practical guide

professional who is trained in Traumatic Birth Recovery (TBR) Three-Step Rewind. They should be able to help you to lift the symptoms that you are experiencing in just three sessions. You can find a list of practitioners at www.traumaticbirthrecovery.com/directories/

In this directory you can find birth professionals who conduct TBR private practice such as doulas and antenatal teachers, but also NHS midwives in some parts of the country. Unfortunately, it is a lottery as to whether your local maternity service offers this. If you are unable to work with a TBR practitioner, then I recommend working through the exercises mentioned earlier in this book.

Be wary of wishing or hoping that these intense, all-consuming feelings will go away or fade with time without the need to do any work yourself. Usually, although not always, treatment or therapy of some kind is needed to deal with the re-triggering nature of trauma symptoms.

Once your levels of anxiety have been lowered and any toxic or heavy feeling lifted from the memory of your last birth, then there is a window of opportunity to begin planning for a different, better birth experience next time.

A personalised birth plan

It is vital that your maternity service is aware that your last experience was traumatic or difficult for you. They need to know how injurious to your emotional health your last birth was, and that this cannot be repeated. To ensure this, they will want to work with you to create a personalised birth plan to avoid another traumatic birth. If you don't tell them, it might not be clear from your notes, and they will not know that they need to handle you with extreme care and compassion. They will have to be informed of how you feel. You may find it difficult to ask for what you want and need. But I would like to reassure you that you are important, that how you feel about your past experience is important, and that you are worthy of being listened to and heard.

A personalised birth plan goes into your hospital notes, meaning that every care provider that you come into contact with during your birth should be aware of it. The best person to help you create a personalised birth plan will usually be a Consultant Midwife or Obstetrician. They can work with you to 'negotiate' a birth plan that is 'outside of guidelines' if necessary. For example, if you are keen to avoid being induced, then let your midwife know so that they can include it in your personalised birth plan.

Recovering from a traumatic birth – a practical guide

It is important to remember that this is *your* body and *your* health. You do not have to compromise your health or bodily integrity for your baby's health or wellbeing. If you encounter any arguments against your desired wishes then ask for clear evidence or a clear explanation of the perceived danger. If you are unhappy with the evidence or the explanation then you can still ask for permission to birth outside of hospital guidelines.

Free birthing

Sometimes there may be valid concerns for the health and wellbeing of you or your baby. Unfortunately, many women have the experience of being coerced and bullied by the phrase 'this is what's best for your baby', and have later regretted their decision because it resulted in injury to their emotional or physical health. This leaves many second-time mothers feeling naturally mistrustful of their care providers. Some women who are unhappy with the lack of support that they have received choose to 'free birth' for their next baby.

Free birthing is when a mother chooses to birth in their own chosen environment without the support or care of maternity services. Counter to popular belief, free birthing is not illegal in the UK. However, many people assume that it is, such is the hold of medical science over our autonomy when it comes to our own physical and emotional health. Unfortunately, many parents consider free birthing to be their only option for birth when they feel unsupported, threatened or unsafe in the hands of maternity services. The growing number of free-birthing parents are a call to maternity services to recognise the long-term damage caused by poor care and its contribution to a traumatic birth experience.

Getting what you need

If you ask for a personalised birth plan and your request is not met favourably, or no reasonable explanation is given as to why your wishes cannot be accommodated, then you may decide to move to a hospital trust with a maternity unit that can accommodate your wishes.

Many parents are unaware that, while there is national guidance from NICE (the National Institute for Clinical Excellence) about many standard hospital protocols, each trust will have their own way of facilitating these guidelines. This covers procedures such as induction, elective C-sections, use of a birth centre, management of gestational diabetes, post-date management, and so on. Each trust will have their own policy on birthing outside of the guidelines too. If you are unable to find support at your local hospital trust, then investigate the option of using a neighbouring trust, as they may well have a different policy.

Even if you do not wish to birth outside of hospital guidelines, then it is still important for your care providers to know if your previous birth experience was traumatising or left a lasting bad memory or heavy feelings. Investigate if your hospital has any additional support that they can offer, such as a trauma informed listening service or TBR Three-Step Rewind from a trained midwife. This can be an opportunity for you to understand your feelings about your last birth, and begin to create a strategy to prevent something similar happening again.

Very often, parents vocalise their feelings and concerns with the midwife at their booking-in appointment. It can feel crushing if this midwife is dismissive or ignorant about the suffering these parents are experiencing as a result of a previous birth. However, this is where talking to a Consultant Midwife can be more appropriate, as they are generally more empathetic, experienced and better-informed about birth trauma and its negative impact on the emotional welfare of mothers and babies. They have the authority to sign off personalised birth plans and they tend to know about additional services like birth listening, TBR Three-Step Rewind, or 'case-loading' midwifery, which aims to provide the mother with continuity of care by the same midwife or group of midwives.

It is understandable that, after one awful experience of maternity care, you might have a very low expectation of the level of care the same hospital can provide next time around. However, in supporting women as a doula, I have often found that when midwives are aware of a woman's poor experience, they are very keen to work towards a healing and positive second experience. All women should have access to kind, compassionate and respectful maternity care, every single time. Sadly, for many reasons this is not always the case. In speaking up about your previous experience and stating what you want for your next birth, you are signalling your refusal to be treated inconsequentially or without proper care this time.

As well as agreeing a personalised birth plan ahead of time with a Consultant Midwife or Obstetrician, you might like to give special consideration to anything in particular that you might find re-triggering. For example, if during your last birth you were told to push for hours on end, then you might wish to express that the word 'push' is not mentioned at you next birth. Instead, may choose to use your own instinct and urge to bring your baby down. Or it might be that you wish to avoid vaginal examinations, if that were a painful feature of your birth trauma. Whatever bad memories you have of your previous birth, then work with your care providers to avoid the experience being repeated.

Choosing the right birth partner

Your partner
Experiencing birth trauma can take a toll on parents' relationships. It's not uncommon for parents to become divided by their experience. Women may feel that their partner didn't advocate for them, defend them or protect

them from unkind care or poor maternity services. Feelings of anger and resentment can resurface in subsequent pregnancies or even when the option of growing the family is discussed.

Discovering that your partner is not the strong, dependable and reliable person that you thought they would be during labour can be a difficult realisation. This can be hard to reconcile or even forgive. Accepting their limitations as a birth partner will provide some space to consider who else you can turn to for support. It can also be healing to acknowledge that your partner may have also found the experience very traumatic but might be hamstrung in communicating their feelings, misbelieving that their feelings are invalid.

Is there a close friend or family member with whom you might feel more at ease and more trusting of during labour? This does not mean having to choose between your baby's father and a good support at your birth. You can have both. Most labour wards and birthing centres will allow two birth partners and this can be very beneficial to both you and your partner. Having two birthing partners means sharing the load; it takes the pressure off your partner, which should, in theory, mean that you get better support.

A doula
Birth doulas provide exactly this kind of support for both women and their birth partner. Doulas can advocate for

Recovering from a traumatic birth – a practical guide

you, if you give them permission to do so. Doulas have a good knowledge of birth, the techniques that may bring you comfort, and what to expect at different stages. Crucially, doulas know how to contain the birthing space so that you can birth in your own way, without worrying about anyone else. The confidence of a good doula in the birth process as a normal physiological event can be contagious, helping you to feel confident too. A doula is so much more than a cheerleader, but ultimately they have your corner and will support you to have the birth that you choose.

You will normally have to pay for a birth doula's services, and fees can range from £800 outside of the capital to £1,500 in London. However, Doula UK, the official organisation representing doulas, has a mentee system for newly trained doulas, meaning that their services may be available at a fraction of these costs.

If you felt unsupported during your last birth, then hiring a doula could be a really good investment. They will stay with you from the time that your labour is established (often even before then) until after your baby is born and you feel ready to be without them. They can help feed, shower and clean you following the birth, and support you to feed your baby too if you need. Birth doulas can provide antenatal education that is often more realistic than other programmes because they have knowledge from the field about how birth works in all settings (home, labour ward and birth centre). Many birth doulas

Recovering from a traumatic birth – a practical guide

have experience of birth trauma either as mothers themselves or vicariously as birth professionals and so they are able to support you compassionately as your pregnancy progresses and your labour approaches.

The birth environment

Ideally you will be able to choose the environment that feels most comfortable for your next birth. Many parents who have experienced traumatic hospital births are understandably unwilling to step back inside a labour ward the second time around. Home birth can feel like an empowering option and one you might like to pursue if your hospital is able to provide a dedicated home-birth midwife. There are many advantages to a home birth when you feel comfortable and secure, not least the feeling of control that people often regain in their own homes.

Pain relief

If you felt that you struggled to cope with pain during your last birth and that it was unbearably uncomfortable then you might benefit from finding out the reason for this. Most women find labour uncomfortable but many are able to manage; when it is unmanageable there is normally a specific reason.

Sometimes, a less than optimum positioning of the baby can make labour very painful, long and tiring. If you were

Recovering from a traumatic birth – a practical guide

denied pain relief or had to wait for it then this will have contributed to your agony and the trauma experienced. If this sounds familiar, then you might benefit from looking into 'optimum foetal positioning' before your next labour. The online authority for this is the website www.spinningbabies.com. Osteopaths who specialise this area can also work with you to help your baby move to an easier birthing position, prior to labour.

Sometimes birth is painful because parents have no resources or techniques to cope with the intensity of discomfort that can come with labour. A good antenatal education programme that teaches breathing and relaxation skills can really help to prepare parents with tools that can be practiced through pregnancy and utilised during birth to ease and manage pain. These relaxation skills can help to lower levels of anxiety and manage worry too. If time or money feel like a barrier to accessing this kind of education, then start with a book or one of the many free online resources that can now be found on the internet.

Sometimes birth is painful because fear and lack of support made it feel intolerable, unsafe and frightening. Again a really good birth support can make all the difference to the experience of pain. When a birthing woman feels safe and secure then pain can become more manageable.

Recovering from a traumatic birth – a practical guide

Lauren's healing birth story

"I just wanted to let you know that Daniel was born at home, in the water, two weeks ago today. It was the most beautiful and healing birth. We did worry that it wouldn't happen – he was 12 days late and predicted to be very large! Fortunately, my midwives were incredible and never once made me feel pressured to change my plans. I had a stop-start early labour for a week beforehand, due to him being back to back and at a funny angle! This was especially frustrating, particularly the night before after a few hours of established labour, during which we'd filled the pool and lit the candles only for it all to stop again! I trusted in my body though, and at 5am things started up again. Pushing started as soon as I got in the pool at 8am and he was born three hours later, weighing in at a healthy 10lb 9oz!! The placenta followed naturally 20 mins later. The first time the midwives laid their hands on me was to help me out of the pool. I hadn't had a single examination or any interference. Just magic! Like I say, it was such a healing birth. It gave me confirmation of what I'd suspected with Ellen's birth, in that if I'd just been allowed more time I wouldn't have required intervention. Thank you so much for giving me the mental tools to do this. I had confidence in myself, and that made every bit of difference."

I hope that the tools in this book are already beginning to support you in your recovery towards emotional health and wellbeing. Remember, they only work if you use them regularly. One of the core components of good emotional wellbeing is becoming consciously aware of

Recovering from a traumatic birth – a practical guide

which thoughts and feelings are holding good mental health at bay. Investing time in this process of conscious awareness can really pay off in the long term. If you can make the time to write a journal about your thoughts and feelings, or have a trusted friend or support person who can comfortably hold space for your thought and feelings to be heard, then this is a great start for maintaining emotional wellbeing. Please be patient with yourself as you undertake this process, use the community group on Facebook, and don't be afraid to seek professional, specialised help if you feel you need it. Above all, remember how you would counsel a friend who had experienced something similar. You would be kind and encouraging, loving and supportive. We all have the ability to be more self-compassionate, it just takes practice.

ABOUT THE AUTHOR

Alexandra Heath is a Clinical Hypnotherapist (Dip Hyp), birth doula and mother of two. She has been listening to parents difficult and traumatic birth stories since 2010 and supporting their recovery when possible. She has a special interest in women's emotional and physical health throughout the perinatal phase and beyond. She lives in Hounslow, West London with her family and a menagerie of pets.

Printed in Great Britain
by Amazon